Bernie Kenny

Isle of Thorns

A collection of poems

First published in 2006

Copyright @ Bernie Kenny 2006

All rights reserved. No part of this publication may be reproduced or transmitted by any means, electronic, mechanical, photocopying or otherwise, without the prior permission of the publisher.

Published by C. Boland, Co. Wicklow.

A CIP catalogue record for this book
is available from the British Library

ISBN 0-9543878-6-4

Cover painting *Dalkey* by Bernie Kenny
Cover design by Carol Boland

Printed and bound in Ireland
by Ruon Print Ltd

In memory of Mike

Acknowledgement is given to the following publications where some of these poems, or versions of them, have appeared:

The Shop
The Stinging Fly

Bernie Kenny lives in Dalkey, Co. Dublin.
She holds an M.A. in Creative Writing (Poetry)
from the University of Lancaster.

Her poems have appeared in *The Shop, Rising Tide,
Wildeside, Away from the Tribe, New Hibernia Review,
Mini Sagas, High Tide* and *The Stinging Fly.*
This is the poet's third collection following *Poulnabrone* ('02)
and *Progeny* ('04).

Gone to Earth, a book of her translations from the Irish poet,
Gréagóir Ó Dúill, was published by Blackmountain Press
in 2005.

Contents

Each diamond day
Ninety Steps	1
Crystal	2
Gold is lonely	3
The linden tree	4
I wake today	5
That was the last time	6
These I have kept	7
See the finches dip and rise	8
In silence now	9
More than glass between us	10
Your gift	11
'Grief'	12
Hedgehog	13
I am the silence	14
I search for signs	15
And what do you think of us now	16

Dandelion clock
The tenth planet	19
Isle of Thorns	20
'There was a child went forth'	21
New Found Out	22
Out of school	23
Fruitfulness	24
Unearthed	25
Possession	26
Endings, beginnings	27
Eighty	28
Eucalyptus	29
Metamorphic woman	30
Coming home	31
Ennis	32
In this photo	33
Shed	34

Water music

Water music	37
Ballroom of Romance	38
A sculpture by Helen O'Connell	39
Soft as terror	40
Their music	41
Pomegranate	42
All eyes	43
Hour upon the stage	44
Remember man	45
Page three	46
Ted and Sylvia	47
Snapshot	48
Home for Christmas 2004	49
A Maori legend	50
December, South Island	52
Kiwi Christmas 2005	53
Spring in her step	54

For their help and encouragement,
I wish to thank Gerald Dawe, Christine Broe,
Nessa O'Mahony and, especially,
The Shed Poets' Society.

Each diamond day

Ninety Steps

The house is still the same,
sun rises on the sea.

Killiney Hill is winter-bare,
walkers take the air.

To Strawberry Hill and back
was our morning routine.

We sat on a low wall
and talked of spring

when you'd be strong again
and we would climb

down all the ninety steps
to Whiterock.

Crystal

Until I held your coldness
in my hands,
stroked the raw edges
of your pain,
felt the weight
of your integrity,
you did not know me.

Gold is lonely

when the moon gilds patterns
on the stillness of the sea

when a field of buttercups
a million goblets of sungleam
is a memory we shared

when light glints glory
on a girl's red-blonde hair

when the yellow rose
you planted for me
in the garden that we made
springs leaves

when three continents
return a family
to mourn
our golden anniversary.

The linden tree

In the unsilent night
I tell myself

that swish is windrush
in the fuchsia bush,
flowers frisking, hiding
red and purple skirts,

that rustle
is veronica stirring.

Alone of its kind
the linden tree
utters tooth-edged
heart-shaped leaves.

Beyond, I hear
the drumming the sea.

I wake today

to raucous wren
ticktocking
eight o'clock
a red sun   and thoughts of you

our pampered cat   forgetting you

the same sea
an icy swim
a tangerine   my prayers for you

counting hours
keeping house
watering   memories of you.

That was the last time

you drove your car, with more than care,
me by your side, quiet, until we reached
Powerscourt, our favourite café.

This time, I bring the tray to our window-table,
leek and potato soup, brown bread
with apricots and sunflower seeds.
For an hour we sit and talk,
praise the Sugarloaf.

I remember our last walk, short, slow, cold.
The coach-house was our goal,
wind whipped white horses on the sea,
we turned home.

And there was one last time
you changed a plug, opened wine,
helped me with the crossword.
Near the end, your solution to a clue
I gave you stays in my mind.
They're not staying at this stage(6).

Exeunt your struggle and your pain.

These I have kept

The wallet from your inside pocket
holds your travel pass.

Because you wore them
through fifty winters,
Dalkey, London, Montreal,
I cannot part with these
Canadian deerskin gloves,
and this not-quite-so-old
tweed cap, 'Shandon Headwear.
Joy and Health to you who wear it'.

I will also keep
these brand-new slippers, my gift,
your size, black leather.
They did not fit your aching feet.

See the finches dip and rise

You stooped over fork and spade,
green fingers sure of when
to plant and pick and prune.
Shrubs shone in pots and beds.

Names tripped off your tongue, scented
sounds of lavender, gardenia, mimosa,
the melody of marigold, campanula,
canterbury bells. Wisteria bloomed
for you – a legacy of pendant blue
charms a house we lived in once.

You knew a hawk from a kestrel
and garden birds by their song,
their feathers, their flight.

The garden lives. I water, weed,
listen and deadhead.

In silence now

two mobile phones
yours and mine
lie side by side

they hold the voice
of fear, of hope
of simulated cheer

goodnights a prayer
goodmornings
another day.

More than glass between us

The naked pane in my new
picture window tells the truth,

your absence is the blaze of sunrise,
daylong loveplay between sea and sky,

pinewood shade on ivied wall,
granite rocks, unwed alpine bed.

Let me live here always,
let me love the world each diamond day.

Your gift

See, there in the photo
a glimpse of jet necklace
and one black earring.

And we were lovely,
smiling a little,
not at each other
but out from the picture,
pensive, pleased
with ourselves so far.

So far distant,
a lifetime ago,
in the new world,

our new world.

'Grief' by Jack B. Yeats

You dip your brush in blue,
indigo, azure, ultramarine,
the clash of steel on steel,
cobalt sky in shreds,
gunsmoke, widows' tears.

You dip your brush in red,
carmine carnage, crimson rage,
rebels running blood,
flames of madder, burnt umber
blast a gable end.

You dip your brush in yellow,
the vitriol of new gamboge,
toxic cadmium, brimstone
stench of smoldering rubble,
the jaundiced eye, fevered pulse.

You dip your brush in green,
olive green.

A Phoenix rises.

Hedgehog

Leaves wear carnival colours
somersault singly into the abyss,
they whisper together, regroup
return together to the earth.

The old and the cold hibernate
squirrels bury nuts
snails seal their shells
hedgehog sleeps alone.

A moth flaps at the window
drawn to shaking morning light.
Autumn's shining sorrow calls
me out to taste the warmth.

I must not be alone when darkness comes.

I am the silence

of mushrooms at dawn,
snowfall, snowdrift, snowmelt,
the lull in the eye of the storm,

level lake holding a mirror to cloud,
every shadow,
oblivious pink in a desert flower,

the Mona Lisa,
a poet's stolen plums in the icebox,
so cold and so sweet,

pickpocket fingers,
bare feet on grass,
black tissue-wrap on a wedding gown.

I am the silence
of voices resting in peace.

I search for signs

Green light drips
on the forest floor,
emeralds moss
and grasses.

I step over roots
stumble through brambles.
Under my feet
a million living things –
minuscule plants
fungi, earthworms
things that fly
scurry and slither –
conspire
to eat one another
fertilize, aerate
create.

And there,
in a shaft of sunlight
laced and new-needled
a larch sapling
stitches spring.

And what do you think of us now?
i.m. Patrick Kenny (1877–1955)

Pride in mother's words
on the back of a photo
of our first Ford van
shines through gold lettering
KENNY'S BAKERY FERBANE.

Nineteen thirty and there am I aged five
scrubbed clean, lined up in smiles
beside three sisters, Nancy, Dodee, Mel.
My shirt, their frocks are Sunday white.
Shoes and fringes shine.

Father, member of the Guild of Master Bakers,
stands to one side, gives us the limelight
as if the hour is ours. That was his style.

See him in his bakehouse, house of flour,
flour in sacks, in scoops, in vats,
flour in pockets, eyebrows, shoes,
flour in clouds and puffs and mounds.

In a white apron, sleeves rolled up,
he works by hand, sets the sponge,
covers, leaves, kneads and kneads,
elbows a dimple on each batch loaf.

Smell the sour-sweet yeast of rising dough,
the hungry crust row on row,
panloaves, duckloaves, turnovers,
sticky glaze on curran'y buns,
pious trays of finger rolls
for the community of Cluny nuns.

Dandelion clock

The tenth planet

Today, Zena, warrior princess,
is added to the solar system
and beyond to trillions
of un-named worlds.

My small home is infatuated with me
and there is nowhere I would rather be.

A window paints the Isle of Thorns,
Saint Begnet's church, sea expanse,
a permanence of Wicklow Hills.

These four rooms have walls enough
to hold my portraits of an absent
family. In their beauty
they keep eyes on me.

Each time I leave I long to return
        down twenty steps
        let myself in
        look out.
        All there
        the sea
        cat sleeping
        petunia drooping
        my universe
rooted in this circle of earth.

Isle of Thorns

Centre stage in an oak tub
the skeleton of a red rose
waits, roots pulsating.

Already, garlic talisman
against blackspot
sends up shoots.

Opportunists,
tetchy nettle, chickweed,
dandelion feed greenly.

Tasting saltsea air, woodland
fungus, frilled oak-brown,
puffs up, clusters and clings.

I'm breathing Dalkey twenty
years and more, in love with
seals, hillwalks, granite stone,

the Vico Road,
the Sugar Loaf,
the Isle of Thorns.

'There was a child went forth' *

and everything she saw and touched,
heard, smelled and dreamt
is part of her:

the yellow walls of a tall house,
love in the lick of a collie's tongue,
sea-holly's silver spikes and flowers,
a parcel in the post, Dick Whittington,
limestone, hazel bush, thistledown,

a robin rigid in her pet cat's claws,
lamp black throwing monsters on the wall,
an avalanche of snowflakes in a paperweight,
panic in bumper-car attack, cackle of sparks,
scorched crimson, electric blue,

hours in a rock pool discovering crabs,
sea-urchins, corkscrewed reflections,
pebbles like gems, fishy smells,
words in her head
            plumduff
  papoose   poppycock
           lilo   lilibolero
    timbuktu
                    tomahawk

time blown away on a dandelion clock.

                              * Walt Whitman

New Found Out

When Atlantic waves on Kilkee strand
wash away sandcastle years,
I learn to swim. My father shows me how.
At New Found Out, off the cliffs and deep,
he talks me in, supports me, lets me go
to panic, dog-paddle, breast-stroke,
earn my wings.

And when the tide is out, Duggerna Reef
gives us the Pollock Holes, rock pools
new-filled and shrill with squeals
of children swimming. We step in
from ledges in fear of brown-black
spines of porcupines. Rain or shine.

Summer after summer
through teenage years,
lavender blue, lavender green,
when I am king you shall be queen.
Sisters, friends, first boyfriends,
dances, heartache, dreams.

To fill the hours we walk the cliffs
past Bishop's Island, by the Diamond Rocks,
the Puffin Hole where we lie prone
and cling in dizzy saltspray gusts.

We shout our loudest in the Amphitheatre,
try snatches of Shakespeare new found out
when Anew Mac Master's strolling players
admit us to their world on mid-summer nights.

Out of school

In the brown mid-city
park, a fountain
is the only sound,

the summer splash
of a childhood stream
tumbling over pebbles.

There we paddled, passed
the hours, shouted when
a trout slid by,

dared forbidden depth,
one of us near drowned,
we didn't tell.

We knew reed warbler
by his song, learned
grey wagtail's yellow

and once, below the bridge,
we caught the bluegreen
flame of a kingfisher.

Fruitfulness

Later she grew them
deliciously
and made end-of-season
green tomato chutney.

The first tomato
my grandmother tasted
was an insult
to her tastebuds.

How could such red ripeness,
lustre, seedy inner flesh
be so new.
Was it vegetable or fruit.

Misunderstood, like
an unpublished poet,
the tomato kept on going
knowing it was first-rate.

Unearthed

A gate creaks open,
morning mist breathes
silence, ivory secrets.

Wet light reveals
one white cap.
A child kneels,

listens, touches
newness, coolness,
satin swell,

lifts it up,
a fairy smell.

Possession

The sea looks in my window
claims as its own
the colours, textures, shapes
I've chosen for this room,
water shades
of grey, cucumber, blue
glass dolphin
wave-sculpted stone
shell's oyster bloom.

Now kind, low lapping,
now fuming,
ocean moods
let themselves in
make themselves felt.

Endings, beginnings

Yet again the pindot blue of speedwell
takes me by surprise

and tireless buttercups open my eyes
as if for the first time.

Pink cushion-heads of thrift are thriving
in this inclement summer.

I slash down nettles and they come
back at me with spite.

Bluebell, vetch and purple loosestrife
are budding, blooming, fading,

nothing finite but my future,
measured and weighed.

My pre-ordained days will melt in
mini-dramas, bus queues, rain,

surprise.

Eighty

As in Bhutan, I extend two hands
to hold my birthday gift,
a cantaloupe, green-yellow gourd.

I press the peel for softness,
network of ridged veins
rough on my skin.

Cut in two, womb-core reveals
glistening seeds,
each ivory oval a nascent universe.

I scoop them out, score fruit flesh
in bite-size pieces dripping juice,
slick, generous, flowery.

Melon,
ripe apple from the Greek melepepon.

Apple,
taste of childhood fusing
green-yellow joy with loss.

Ripe apples windfall on trodden grass
as autumn slipslides into winter.

Eucalyptus

She breathes in perfume
of now, of down-under, of childhood.

On Killiney Hill she stoops,
picks up an empty seed case,
woody chalice.
Frail fingers trace texture
of cross-ridged top,
cross hollowed underneath,
eyes follow lean length of trunk,
peeling bark, straggle of branches,
wilt of leaves.

She walks among trees,
among scratching and breathing,
squawking and making.
Koalas cling to branches,
feed on leaves.
Raucous laugh reveals
a Kookaburra camouflaged,
stock-still, on the lookout for a meal.
In vastness of space evergreens rise.
They survive fire, regenerate,
fill the bush with births, re-births
and wide-awake, rainrinsed smells.

A phial of blue glass,
sprinkle of oil,
tingle of scent,
gentleness,
learning to spell
a new grown-up word.

Metamorphic woman

Older than the Cailleach Béara she stands
foot-tall on my rosewood table
beside the ticking clock.

In a guttural rumble of shale,
a scatter of sheep, I found her
glinting on white mountain heather.

A rugged rock, fragile as a flower,
I lift her up, take her pulse.
Blood of ancient words runs in her veins.

Sealed lips hold a history
of earth's core, of clay and tactile
water compacting pleasure, pain.

In pleated watersilk and amber
time enfolds her secrets.
She catches the light.

Coming home

I swim against tide rush,
fix my sights above
green hiss of foam,
leap one last boulder,
land, exultant and exhausted
in the stream where I was born.

For three infant years
this riverbed is home to me
until seafever in my genes
propels me – a small smolt
in new seacoat of silver –
through unknown salty depths.

One among hundreds
in our straggling school,
the current ferries me
offers rich food. Shrimps
turn my white flesh pink.
I gorge on herring
hold and crush it with my jaws,
swallow it headfirst.

To fulfil my destiny
ancestral memory
guides my homing path.
Without food or sleep I drive
myself in sinuous lengths,
fight rapids, scale waterfalls
with eagerness of one newborn.

Ennis

I am welcome for a while
to holiday in my home town.
My uprooted roots are steadfast,
at times like this in the sun
they thirst for a rose-tinted past.

These lanes, this sky, church bells
were once all mine,
sugar and gossip across the wall,
feuds old as Clare limestone,
a banner of yellow and blue.

A local by birthright
in a world that was locked
and easy, I knew who was who.

Never having left, never having come,
locals tend the garden.
I look on.

In this photo

I'm dipping six-year-old toes
in a rock pool, our rock pool,
pitted out of limestone
at the edge of the Atlantic.

Sepia drowns the colours
of wide-eyed childhood
scouting, shouting, raiding,
never lost for names.

Apart from periwinkles
shells are shells, whether
butter-yellow, purple, pink
or silky brown like chestnuts.

Sea urchins
lurk under ledges
bare black spines at us,
we call them porcupines

and sea anemones
plum-red blobs
are bloodsuckers,
bloodfull
           lovely
                    scary.

Shed

This room, a summer-house,
celebrates the sea in pebbles, shells,
paintings of boats, lobsterpots,
a dolphin etched on Shanagarry dish,
the only sound a ticking
and, from outside, the squawk
of gull and children at Whiterock.

A mirror looks through the glass door,
frames a rockery, nasturtium gold,
ribbon of white sea, the Sugarloaf
and pink promise in a strip of
evening sky.

Around me, gifts, purchases, beachcombed
oddities make poems of who, where, when.
Conch hears the waves at Port of Spain
clock ticks Camden Market, Camden Lock
and, full of themselves, seastones sit there
high and dry.

Pinned to the wall, a postcard shows
the Dylan Thomas writing shed
in creative disarray. As my good night
draws near I hear his voice.

To go gentle would be my choice.

Water music

Water music

Wet-in-wet a sable brush
rains a grey crescendo
on colours swirling home.

Yellow mists a halo over purple.
Orange sings to blue and blue.

Stippling a refrain
they listen to the rippledrip
of minims on the silver path,

catch themselves
in puddles   dancing.

Ballroom of Romance

Girls of all ages, in smiles
and flower-print dresses,
sit side by side on benches

shyly watching
boys of all ages stand
shyly watching them.

Everybody loves somebody sometime.
The band strikes up.
Boy chooses girl. On with the dance.

Has she grown too old to dream.
Has she, in twenty years, waltzed
away her youth, her beauty, her need.

Must she save the last dance
for whiskey kisses
and a moot proposal

under a mocking moon.

A sculpture by Helen O'Connell

Luminous in marble
skintint delicately veined
Badu is all woman,

her hair a turbaned pile
she wears a pendant amulet
a Mona Lisa smile.

I look long, longingly
disobey the sign.
With full palm, fingers splayed,

I stroke the mound
where love lives,
her belly great with child.

Soft as terror

I wake to noise moving
through rooms in the night.

Rigid I rise, turn on lights,
freeze when fur brushes my feet.

A stray, unafraid, purrs a plea
to stay. With a saucer of milk

a coward lures her out,
turns the key in the lock.

Their music

High in the blue air
from dawn to sundown
there is croaking.

In crowns of tree-clumps
beaks and claws build
and patch jangled nests.

Like witches' brooms
a murder of rag-feathers
swoops on ploughed field

or waddles
in staccato hops
along grub-rich ditches.

Windrocked in scratchy
cradles, hatchlings screech
for masticated seeds

and all the while
raucous caws squawk
warcries, lovecalls, warnings,

joy at being crows,
so black
so tuneful.

Pomegranate

Faithless tree
blazons red-yellow suns.

Man and woman inhale
sweetness they desire
but dare not.

Tree of knowledge, tree of wisdom.
Eat
hisses in the creeping vines.

Pride plucked, possessed,
they share bitter flesh
spit blood-red seeds.

All eyes

On sunwarmed roof of the garden shed
she stretches her elegant length,
silk-furred, slit-eyed, hour after hour,
ready to pounce, wrens on her mind.

A shiver in the fuchsia bush,
dart and dive of a stump tail
strip her civilized veneer.
Alert, twitching, she waits,
atavistic fire in her green eyes.

On fuse wire feet a clockwork flurry
beaks and scratches for beetles
and seeds, spies danger
in the gunsight of an eye,
flickers, disappears.

Hour upon the stage

On a granite boulder
feldspar and quartz
play minor roles
when sunshine
spotlights
a mica fragment
and sparkles it
to stardom.

Remember man

We are old. Of stars, bits of planets,
bomb-blasts, ancestors' bones,
loved only when we are of gold.

Erosion, flowers, decay bring us to life.
We ride the wind, gadabout on sunrays,
muddy drains, settle anywhere.
Softly we gather in attic and cellar
on discarded things, on treasure.

You remove us from your ticking clock,
shake us out. You cannot wipe us out.
Billions of us. We shall inherit the earth.

Page three

On the last
day of May
I learn from
a picture
in the paper
that yesterday
in a meadow
near the town
of Bensheim
Germany
a ladybird
was spotted
scrambling
down the stem
of a poppy.

Ted and Sylvia

Years after death he sketched
her in letters, again and again,
in shades of her shining,
her new agony, old despair.

He sees her slim, naked and new,
long American legs, winged fingers
a hummingbird dance, hair
floppy-blond and that filmstar bang.

Named after salvias, red was her
colour, lavish burgundy velvet,
frail poppies for warming the dead,
everything white defeated and
splashed with roses, catastrophic red.

At the altar on Bloomsday
in a pink knitted dress
she brimmed with God,
the heavens showed riches
and nothing was smudged.

Snapshot

Two
grey herons
stand
hunched
one
behind
the other.
They wait,
white necks
shape an s,
yellow
dagger-bills
plot
a swallow-dive.

Home for Christmas 2004
for Helen and Ciaran

From Maori Land of the Long White Cloud,
land of sunshine and of deluge,

they come with gifts,
two kilos of Otago cherries.

In a crystal bowl, the fragrant fruit
blends sunset shades of rose and gold.

Among the holly and the ivy
it makes itself at home.

Satin skin snaps between our teeth,
honeyed flesh melts on our tongues.

Twelve thousand miles
divide us once again.

A greater gift remains.

A Maori legend

For long ages, in The Great Nothingness,
Skyfather, Ranginui, lies in the arms
of Earthmother, Papatuanuka. They hug
and darkness wraps love around them.

Their children grope in cold tunnels,
safe, but yearning for space.
In vain, each childgod tries
to prise his parents apart

until Tane-Mahuta, god of trees,
birds, insects, gathers his strength,
thrusts his father skywards, far
from his beloved. Ranginui bleeds.

As he loosens his embrace, moans
rumble through Papatuanuka.
Space opens between them. The god
of storms blasts darkness away

and in celestial light her children
see their mother, a loveliness undreamed.
She grieves. Her love for Ranginui
rises on dawn mist. He rains seas of tears.

To adorn his father, Tane moves
into the unknown, finds The Shining Ones,
piles them, dazzling, in a basket
to fasten to the mantle of the sky.

At night Ranginui shakes out his robe,
Marama hangs her golden globe,
the heavens fill with the twinkle
and glow of a thousand eyes.

Out of warm red-ochre soil
the gods form a woman. Tane
breathes life into her and she is
soft, sun kissed, brimming delight.

Tane loves her, names her Hine.
Their children people the earth.

December, South Island

A rough-hewn monument proclaims
The Fortyfifth Parallel and I am there,
vertical, in a flowered summer dress,
half-way down the world.

As a memento I pick up a stone, curve
fingers round it, feel my life drawn into
its snowwhite stillness. Here only once
in the glass-clear air, I have it all
before me, this vastness, this scenery.

Light spreads like wings, fans sunbaked
colour into everything. At my feet, the pink,
grey-green and lavender of lichens scab rocks.
A canyon plunges drunkenly and the creek
named after Roaring Meg foams fury.

Sombre bush and tussock reach the blue
of a never-ending lake. Sky expands.
With names to suit their height,
Moonraker, Stargazer, Mount Aspiring,
distant peaks throw titanic shadows.

A sudden southerly stings. I leave
for Wanaka to wallow in a thermal pool.
At Lake Wakatipu holiday traffic halts
while four ducks walk across the road.

Kiwi Christmas 2005

I leave
frost splintering blueblack day,
one last geranium, Christmas
spangling children's eyes,
a crescent moon, Venus at her
brightest above Killiney Bay.

I find
a welcome in The Land
of the Long White Cloud,
summer sun on lotus flower,
on agapanthus blazing blue,
summer rain root-reaching,
greening, working at full steam.

Christmas is a barbeque,
a cherry orchard drooping
lustrous joy, the bell-like notes
or guttural squawk of tui bird,
pohutakawa tree aflame
with blossom-baubles.

Night turns on new constellations,
children in their dressing-gowns
tiptoe through fairy lights
on Franklin Road and Santa's
on his way from the South Pole.

Spring in her step

Weave me a dress to dance in
on wintery nights, a wide
gypsy skirt that swishes
the ripple of reeds in the lake

cloudsoft, light as swansdown caress
purple of loosestrife, blueberry, heather
shimmer of goldrust on fern frond
whirl of leaves crimson and bronze

flowers in her auburn hair.